T0370500

A Summer in Yellowstone

Ron Gabriel

A Summer in Yellowstone

iUniverse books may be ordered through booksellers or by contacting:

iUniverse
1663 Liberty Drive
Bloomington, IN 47403
www.iuniverse.com
1-800-Authors (1-800-288-4677)

Because of the dynamic nature of the Internet, any web addresses or links contained in this book may have changed since publication and may no longer be valid. The views expressed in this work are solely those of the author and do not necessarily reflect the views of the publisher, and the publisher hereby disclaims any responsibility for them.

Any people depicted in stock imagery provided by Getty Images are models, and such images are being used for illustrative purposes only.
Certain stock imagery © Getty Images.

ISBN: 978-1-5320-8007-4 (sc)
ISBN: 978-1-5320-8008-1 (hc)
ISBN: 978-1-5320-8009-8 (e)

Library of Congress Control Number: 2019911747

Print information available on the last page.

iUniverse rev. date: 09/16/2019

THIS BOOK IS DEDICATED

TO

YELLOWSTONE NATIONAL PARK

TRULY A NATIONAL TREASURE

Oh give me a home where the bison roam.

INTRODUCTION

I woke up one morning and said to myself,
"Where am I?"

The answer came back immediately,
"Yellowstone."

"How did I get here?"

"You drove."

"But why am I here?"

"You have suffered all your life from wanderlust. There is no cure.
The doctors have no magical pill to control this condition.'

"But I am too old for all this."

"That's what everyone thinks."

CONTENTS

ADDENDUM

THE FOLLOWING STORIES ARE NOT ABOUT YELLOWSTONE.
THESE VINGETTES COVER GLIMPSES AND RAMBLINGS OF THE
LIFE AND TIMES OF THE AUTHOR

HOW IT ALL BEGAN

While wintering in St Petersburg, Florida, we knew a couple that had worked in Yellowstone National Park for eight continuous summers. I was envious of their experience and thought, "That would be a fun adventure, like a paid vacation."

Flash forward to the year 2018. In January, I googled, "Seasonal jobs in Yellowstone National Park." I refined the search from there. It came down to two companies: Delaware North and Xanterra. Both companies had positions available all over Yellowstone, Old Faithful, Lake, Canyon, Mammoth, Grant Village and Fishing Bridge.

About this time in the process, I thought it prudent to check with my life's partner. She was not against this whole adventure/dream of mine. I did point out the positives, no cooking for the time in Yellowstone, no housework and no grocery shopping for the summer.

I phoned Florida and asked our friend, "Where is the best place to work in Yellowstone?" Her reply came back quickly, "Grant Village."

Applying was not easy. Xanterra had gone green. This means everything must be done on the computer Yours truly, would never be mistaken for a "nerd." It took us a month before we received the word that we were hired. Before the word came, a young man named Tom interviewed us by phone. Tom warned us that Yellowstone was very rural. The wi fi is not the best. He wanted us to think it over before committing. We told him that we understood but were still excited about the opportunity of spending a, "Summer in Yellowstone."

To complete our hiring, we needed two letterers of recommendation for each of us. It was not supposed to be a family member. Who would we ask? After some phone calls, some twisting of arms, we miraculously came up with our recommendations.

So, after all this, we figured we were home free. No, our buddy Tom phoned and said we would have to have a credit check. What, were we buying a house? Tom said, "Xanterra would pay for the credit check." A company out of New York City contacted us by e mail of course. Does anyone use the United States Post Office anymore? We sent them the information they requested and after a couple of weeks, we were approved to work in Yellowstone for the fourth time.

We were to check in at Gardiner Wyoming on May 17, 2018. Our contract would run from May 17 to October 4th, so it would be a long summer in Yellowstone.

ON BEING AN OCTAGENARIAN

The first thing about being eighty-ish is that you are so grateful just to be here. You know many people that haven't made it this far. Every day is like a gift: the bright colorful flowers, a sunny clear blue sky and the joy of the closeness of family and friends. If your health is good that's the key. You can make your own happiness.

The eighties do have some advantages. You have the advantage of the "The Eighties Card." You can't charge anything on it but it's better than a "Get out of jail FREE card." The way it works say the "light of your life" grandson asked you to go hiking along a snake infested river where squadrons of blood thirsty mosquitoes hover about. You inform him that you are after all over eighty now, so you better stay home and watch reruns of Lawrence Welk. He will ask "Who is Lawrence Welk?" You will overlook this because he probably doesn't know who Matt Dillon is either. Another example of where "The Eighties Card" comes in handy would be: A big family trip is being planned to the local zoo. They are going to walk around on a hot day and view all the smelly animals in their restricted cages. So out comes "The Eighties Card." You say, "As much as I would like to go to the crowded zoo with the family, I had better beg off. At "MY AGE," who knows what might happen?"

There are really many benefits to being eighty. No one asks you to help them move furniture or pour concrete and you are only asked to babysit as a last resort. My dear wife of fifty-six years does not want me on a ladder anymore. So, I sufferingly say, "OK darling, if that's what you want." Between you and me ladders are for working people. That is now way above my pay grade anyhow.

When you arrive in your eighties, you automatically become a member in good standing of "The Eighties Club." You develop a kinship with other octogenarians.

When you meet there is an instant bond. They, (like you) have traversed the long sometimes dangerous road to arrive here and mutual respect is shown. You have shared memories of an era gone by and mostly forgotten and you both know it personally. It is said, "When an old man dies, a library burns to the ground." To be politically correct one should say, 'When an old person dies, a library burns to the ground." Somehow that does not have the same ring.

One thing that all of us in our eighties have in common is that we grew up listening to the radio. Television did not become popular until we were in our teens. All of us can tell you when and where we saw our first television set. Who among us can forget, The Shadow, Henry Aldridge, The Great Gildersleeve or The Lone Ranger? "Hi Ho Silver, getem up Scout."

In later years my hearing has decreased. I do not always hear all that is said. You know, that's not all bad.

At eighty some would say we are grouchy and opinionated. I believe that is expected and should be overlooked. Certain subjects should not be brought up: the Government, the high cost of everything or how bad us eighty-year olds had it as a kid. You already know that we had to walk to school in all kinds of weather and it was up hill both ways.

One of the revelations of "Olddom," we regretfully admit, we have not discovered all the mysteries or secrets of life. Tune in next year, we may have a revelation, who knows.

By the way, at eighty, youth treats us with a little more respect and sometimes even listens to our stories, if we keep them short. We still have not reached the age where we are asked, "What do you attribute your long life to?" I think that comes at ninety.

The older we get the faster life flies by. Christmas, Valentine's Day, Memorial Day, Fourth of July, Labor Day and Thanksgiving go by like a speeding car. Birthdays are the worst; seems like every month we add another year to our life. We have lost some of our lifelong friends along the way. We become acutely aware that lifelong friends are irreplaceable. But life moves on carrying us along with it.

So now that you have read this diatribe, you should be more aware of how to approach someone of our generation. "How you are doing old timer" does not make it. Try, "Hey handsome, (or beautiful) you're looking good today." After that opening, we are putty in your hands.

THE LONG ROAD WEST

One thing I learned as we prepared to leave for Montana, is that the longer you are going to be gone the harder it is to get away. There is mail to forward, newspaper to cancel, fish to find a sitter for, caretaker for the flowers, pay the yard man for months in advance, see that the utilities are automatically deducted and much more. Is it any wonder people shy away from traveling?

I had a new set of tires put on the Honda. Nothing gives a man more peace of mind then a new set of tires.

Google related that the trip west would be over twenty- five hundred miles. We decided to take five days to Livingston, Montana and then take a day to rest up. The next day on the nineteenth of May, we would drive the fifty -three miles to Gardner Wyoming to Xanterra's offices. There we would have to sign all the papers for our work summer and be issued our uniforms.

We blasted off Friday, May 12th. We lodged at a Best Western in Tennessee on the first night. We thought this very fitting, "Best Western" heading West. The next night we stayed in Peoria, Illinois. We were thrilled to find a Bob Evans Restaurant as we don't have any in the Low Country of South Carolina. We feasted on food we had not eaten in a long time. We overdid it but travel makes one hungry.

A couple years ago, all the hotels and motels changed the size of their pillows. They now have four small pillows rather than two large pillows I wonder what happened to all the big pillows? Are they in our landfills all over the country? Some people like their pillows so much that they take them on vacation with them. I am not that fond of my pillow. It can stay home.

Enough about pillows, back to our Western trek. From Peoria we drove to Spencer Iowa. My wife had read a book about a cat named Dewey. Dewey was found as a baby kitten in the drop box at the library in Spencer, Iowa. It was a super cold morning. The librarian took it in and named it Dewey after Dewey Decimal System.

Dewey became famous. He greeted everyone at the door and was a permanent fixture around the library. In 2008, the librarian, Vicki Myron wrote a book about Dewey. The book made him even more famous. A television crew from Japan came and did a film story all about Dewey. I am sad to say Dewey is no longer with us, having passed away at the age of nineteen. There are many pictures of him on the walls of the library and a ceramic wall in his honor in a local park.

We visited the library and the park with the ceramic wall. This was part of my commitment package to my wife to get her to Yellowstone. She asks, "Honey, can we stop at Spencer, Iowa?" I replied, "Of course darling, sounds like fun." I have been married 56 years. Can you tell?

The fourth night on the road, we stayed in Rapid City, South Dakota. We were in the Black Hills twenty-seven miles from Mt Rushmore. This Black Hills area is sacred to the Indians who have lived here for generations. There is a huge sculpture of Crazy Horse on a mountain near here. It's not finished yet. The government offered to pay to finish the impressive carving. The Indians refused.

Deadwood South Dakota is forty-one miles away. Wild Bill Hickok was shot there on August 7, 1886. He was thirty-nine years old. Legend has it that he was playing poker and his hand was aces and eights. But what was the fifth card?

We arrived in Livingston, Montana, on Tuesday May 17, after driving 2,376 miles in five days. The elevation in Livingston is 4,500 feet above sea level. We wanted to rest up in Livingston and adjust to the elevation.

On Thursday, May 17, 2018, we drove the fifty some miles to Gardiner Montana. The Northern gate to Yellowstone. We checked in, signed all the papers and received our summer work uniforms.

The drive from Gardiner to Grant Village was seventy- four miles. The drive to Grant Village was spectacular. There was still snow along the roads and in the mountains. The blue sky with white capped mountains and the Yellowstone River winding down in the canyons along the valley floor were breath taking.

We decided, even if we didn't stay in Yellowstone for the summer, this drive was worth the long road west.

THE ROOSEVELT ARCH

The Roosevelt Arch is just South of Gardiner, Montana. It is the North entrance into Yellowstone. The Arch was constructed of large stone in 1902 and 1903. The Arch itself is fifty feet high and twenty feet across. Inscribed on the top of this edifice is:

"For the Benefit and Enjoyment of the People."

The corner stone was dedicated April 23, 1903 by the President of the United States, Teddy Roosevelt. He was on a two-week camping outing in the Park. The President had as few people around him as possible because he wanted to experience the pristine and solitude of Yellowstone.

I have always felt a kinship with Teddy Roosevelt.

I portrayed him in the play, "Arsenic and Old Lace," in high school. The more I have read about him, the more fascinating he becomes. He was President, he enlisted the Rough Riders and he spearheaded the Panama Canal, just to name a few things that he did.

Yellowstone was dedicated a National Park in 1872 by Ulysses S. Grant, the President at that time. The Park was the first National Park in the world. The Congress, Senate and President had great foresight in preserving 2.2 million acres for the generations yet to come.

In August of 1886, the Army rode into Yellowstone to protect it from poaching, vandalism, corporate greed and the tourist that longed to see the Park. The Army and most of the people that came to Yellowstone came by train to Gardiner, Montana. The tourists got around the Park in stagecoaches. The Army constructed Fort Yellowstone. The fort was not like the forts you see in the movies. The Army built big sturdy stone structures. Thirty-five of those buildings are still standing thanks to the preservation program of the National Parks Service. The Army finally left Yellowstone in 1918 after a job well done.

The major areas of the Park are Mammoth Hot Springs, Old Faithful, Grant Village, Roosevelt, Lake, Canyon and Fishing Bridge. The cost to stay at one of these Lodges ranges around $250.00 to $350.00 per night. That is without air conditioning or Wi-Fi. Many visitors stay outside Yellowstone at West Yellowstone, Cody, and Jackson, Wyoming, or Gardiner, Montana. The room rates are more reasonable and they are still close to the Park.

The time we were in Yellowstone we saw very few semi-trucks on the roads which was a treat. There were many campers and motorcyclist and a few hardy bicyclists which mingled with the huge influx of tourist vehicles.

I met an older couple in the dining room who were biking from Seattle to Key West. They were a friendly couple who I admired for their gumption.

The roads in Yellowstone are all serpentine and the elevation can vary in altitude over a thousand feet. The roads have very narrow berms so driving or biking in the Park can be dangerous. Thirty-five miles an hour is the usual top speed. When a tourist sees a bear, elk, moose or bison, they stop wherever they are, even the middle of the road. It seems that most tourists feel that these wild animals are cuddly and friendly. The first thing the tourists want to do after spotting a wild animal is get as close as they can to snap a picture.

A tourist asked me one evening in the dining room, "What's the best place to see in Yellowstone?" After I thought about the question for a few moments, my reply was, "Just driving through the Park with all its spectacular scenery spawns gratefulness just to be here."

THE DEATH MARCH

The first evening we were in Yellowstone, Tom, our group trainer, walked the group of newbies around Grant Village. The altitude was 7,733 feet above sea level. We encountered snow on the walking paths and piles of snow in the parking lots where it had been plowed aside.

First, Tom marched us over to the Employees Dining Room. From this point forth it will be referred to as the EDR. The hike to the EDR was around a half a mile. Tom explained as we trudged along huffing and puffing that bears had been seen in this area. Also, mother elks like to have their calf's here and hide their young among the trees. He went on to say, "Don't mess with mother elks. They are very protective of their young calf." Before my tired legs and withered lungs arrived at the now called EDR, I decided that we would be driving to all our meals.

After supper, Tom continued his grueling walking tour of Grant Village. We visited the Post Office, the Registration Building, the Lake House, (a restaurant that sets right on Lake Yellowstone) and the General Store run by Delaware North which was not open yet. Tom finally lead us back to our dorm.

By the way the younger ones on our excursion did not seem to mind. They walked briskly from place to place and frolicked in the snow. I despised their joyfulness by the time we crawled back to the dorm.

THE DORM

On our first day, we were assigned a room on the second floor. The stairs would be a challenge for us the whole summer due to the altitude. The room had its own bath which surprised us. We were expecting to walk down the hall to the bathroom. There were two twin beds, a small closet, and the bathroom sink was in the main room with the shower/tub and toilet in a smaller room.

The dorm had a large lobby open from the first floor lobby to the second-floor ceiling. On the first floor was a pool and foosball tables along with chairs and tables arranged for conversations or games. The second floor had an open balcony containing a ping pong table, weight room, an area for two computers and various card size tables. The second floor lobby was a quiet place to sit and read or write post cards. I kept a journal while we were there. The second-floor lobby was a perfect place for journal writing when I did not have to work.

Down the hall next to the second-floor lobby was a laundry room we could use for free. There were six washers and dryers. See the picture of the directions for the laundry. The picture gives you an idea of our varied group.

The dormitory had a pleasant atmosphere. Girls and guys from different countries hanging out in the lobby talking and laughing. Movies were shown on different nights of the week. Every other Wednesday night was an employee get together with free ice cream. My favorite was huckleberry.

The one drawback to the dorm was the lock on our door. To lock or unlock the door we had to jiggle the key until the lock decided to respond. If we were leaving or coming back to our room and we had our arms full, the lock refused to respond until till we put all the items down on the floor. Then and only then would the lock entertain the idea of opening. The lock also played favors; it didn't like my wife.

The dorm was our home away from home for the summer. Our neighbors were mostly quiet. Sometimes the cute, little giggly Asian girls got a kick out of yelling down the hall in the middle of the night to hear the echo. On not so rare occasions when the Pub (Employees bar) closed at 2:00am happy voices resounded through the quiet night.

All in all the dorm was a fun place with young laughter and voices of many nationalities echoing through the halls and lobby. Those memories of the people we encountered and the conversations we had with them will not soon be forgotten.

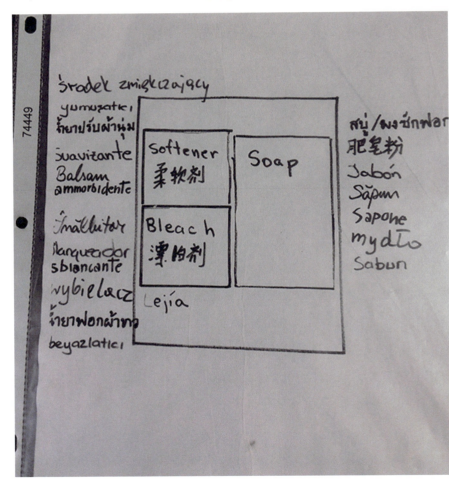

Instructions in the laundry room of the dorm.

THE GRANT VILLAGE DINNING ROOM

Sunrise over Lake Yellowstone.

The Grant Village Dining Room, where I worked, has floor to ceiling windows looking out on Lake Yellowstone. The lake is the largest alpine lake in the world above seven thousand feet. When the restaurant opened in late May, the view was awesome with the blue water of the lake and bordered by the green pine trees and the distant snowcapped mountains.

The dining room opened at 6:30am. It was always a treat to view the sunrise over Lake Yellowstone. All the guests clamored for the tables next to the windows even in the evening when it was dark.

My job as host was to carry the menus and escort the customers to their assigned tables. We had to clock in at 6:15am. There was always a little staff meeting where our supervisors kept us currant on our responsibilities and duties. The morning shift lasted until 11:00am for the hosts and longer for the severs. The dining room closed at 10:00am but Xanterra prided themselves in never turning away a hungry person. Having said that, no additional customers were allowed in after 10:05 sharp.

The evening hours were 5:00pm until 10:00 pm. The staff was always amazed at the number of families who showed up hungry between 9:30pm and 10:00pm. They had children too. What were they doing from 5:00pm until 10:00pm?

Over fifty percent of the dining room clientele were Oriental. Around twenty percent were from India. Many came to the restaurant speaking little or no English. Usually there was a younger person in the group that did all the translating. Luckily, we had a server and assistant server from China. When I seated one of these Englishless tables, I would hurriedly find our Chinese translator. It was a kick to hear the whole table break out in conversation when they found someone who understood them.

An older French couple came in. I talked to them some as I escorted them to their table. We were trained to do this plus make eye contact. After a while the gentleman motioned me back over to their table. He said, "My wife and I have been discussing, who is the older, you or me?" I told him I was eighty- three. He proudly replied, "I am eighty- six." His wife chirped in happily, "I'm eighty-three." They said they were from Israel. I replied that I thought that was wonderful. The man asked, "Why." I said that I always admired the tradition and history of the Jewish race. After our brief conversation I began to wonder if I stand out as being older here in the dining room more than I thought.

We had servers and servers' assistants, not waiters, waitresses or busboys. Of course, now it's probably bus person.

One evening, one of the servers and I were in the busy kitchen. For some reason we broke into the song, "Mercedes Benz," by Janis Joplin.

"Oh Lord won't you buy me a Mercedes Benz
My friends all drive Porches
I must make amends
Worked hard all my lifetime
No help from my friends
Oh Lord won't you buy me a Mercedes Benz"

It was fun I always liked that song. I was surprised that the server, being young, knew the words.

He seemed surprised that an old man like me knew the song. If any of the other staff in the kitchen at the time were impressed, they never let on. The server, let's call him Aaron, claimed to be from Indiana and Tennessee. He could charm the socks off the guests at his tables, when he wanted to. He frequented "The Seven Stool Saloon" to do his drinking, which was expensive. He also liked to eat in the Grant Village Dining Room on some of his nights off. I hoped that he would have enough money left over to get back to Tennessee in the fall.

Later in the summer, Aaron was eating in the dining room with a group of friends and some staff members from our dining room along with an off-duty supervisor. He motioned me over to his table and we sang a command performance of "Mercedes Benz" for the group and nearby tables. There was no applause when we finished. The lack of applause did not bother us at all because when you know you're good, you don't need that validation.

Restaurant work is physically demanding. You don't have much to contribute if you are in "creeper" mode. The whole shift, you are on your feet and hustling. Early in the summer, I continually suffered from leg cramps or Charlie horses as we used to refer to them. Hot pads and Motrin were my relief. All of us were advised to drink plenty of water. Everyone carried a water container. I Finally had to phone my doctor. She sent out a statement saying I could only work one shift a day. All went well from then on. I still had to work what was lamentably called, "The turn around." That was working the evening shift until close at 11:00pm, then coming back in the next morning at 6:15am. It wasn't much fun, but I proudly survived.

Most of the older patrons that came into the dining room and saw me were interested in how I got here. I would launch into my pet spiel on, how I got to Yellowstone, how I came out of retirement in South Carolina, how my wife and I are working here for the summer and how we get two days a week off together so we can tour around the area. Usually I had a captive audience and received some glances of admiration which I enjoyed.

I have many fond memories of the gang I worked with and the guests we served in the Grant Village Dining Room. Thanks, Xanterra.

TYLER

Tyler was one of the supervisors in The Grant Village Dining Room. He was good at his job because he knew instinctively who was behind and needed his assistance. He would help at the host's front desk, when we needed him. Being tall, he could see over the six-foot wall separating the entrance area from the dining room. From his vantage point, he could easily see which tables were available for the seating of patrons. The rest of us had to grab a pencil and paper and scurry around the wall into the dining room to see which were available. Tyler bused tables carried food trays and got drink orders. He was everywhere.

Supervision is a tricky job. You want to be liked but you can't be one of the group. You learn a lot about yourself when you become a supervisor. I personally was not a good supervisor because I thought if I lead by example that would show them how it should be done. John Wayne said about leadership, "Find out which way they are going and get in front of them."

We, the dining room staff, always breathed a sigh of relief when we heard the word that Tyler was on our shift. Supervision is a gift and Tyler had it in spades. He could even bridge that precipice and become one of us. I can't remember getting a direct order from Tyler all summer. He would say, "Ron, do you want to find some menus?" or "Ron, do you want to help move the tables?" One of Tyler's specialties was moving tables to accommodate large groups of eight to fifteen. Moving tables was not my forte. I would pull, push and grunt but those nasty tables refused to budge. Even the girl servers could seem to move those tables effortlessly. Annette was better at moving those dastardly tables then me. One morning, as I was leaving at the end of my shift, Tyler jokingly said, "Ron, I thought you were going to hang around and help move some tables."

The rumor was that Tyler graduated from Indiana University with an electrical engineering degree. He must have taken a class in moving tables while he was there.

Tyler liked to hike in Yellowstone. One stormy night on his way back to the dorm, his small red truck slide off the road and down the mountain side for a way. Luckily the truck stayed upright, and Tyler crawled out unhurt. The truck was undamaged also, but Tyler said, "It ran a little loud after that."

One evening in the dining room we were super busy. People were lined up out to the entrance door. We had just seated a table when we looked up and they had moved to another table without asking. Then they moved again while we were watching them. Tyler happened to be hanging out at the host desk. He too watched the people move and all he said was, "That's rude." The rest of us were thinking a little stronger language. For Annette and I, from that time on for the rest of the summer "that's rude" was the key response when either the staff or guests did something we didn't like.

Tyler was promoted to a position way up in Mammoth. He would have his own office and the use of a company car. Don't you just love it when good things happen to nice people?

I did feel sorry for the dining room staff because Tyler and I left about the same time. How was the restaurant supposed to function without either of us?

OLD FAITHFUL

There she goes again. What a gal!

Everyone that tours Yellowstone must see Old Faithful. There is an unfounded rumor that when you exit Yellowstone Park a Ranger will ask, "Have you seen Old Faithful?" If you say, "No," the Ranger refuses to let you out.

The best way to see Old Faithful is to go to the Old Faithful Inn. It is a huge log structure built in 1903. Robert Reamer was the architect.

The lobby of the Inn rises unobstructed eighty foot to the roof. There are second and third floor balconies that look down on the lobby floor. A gigantic stone fireplace dominates the center of the Inn.

The object is to arrive after Old Faithful has erupted. Then you have an hour to be in place for the next show. You now have time to walk around, take in the beauty of the historic structure, and browse the gift shop. The next step is to take the stairs to the second-floor balcony, get yourself a drink or better yet a big dish of huckleberry ice cream. Off the second-floor balcony is an outside deck that has the very best view of Old Faithful. You then find a good viewing seat, drink your drink, eat your ice cream and tell yourself how lucky you are to be here in Yellowstone ready to see one of America's great treasurers. When Old Faithful goes up, you take your pictures to show your friends and neighbors back home that you were here. Just remember, they don't care.

A lesson to live by. My wife was a huge Elvis fan. One year she and a few of her girlfriends made the pilgrimage to Graceland in Memphis Tennessee. My wife, while walking through the rooms that Elvis lived in, took many pictures to have a remembrance of this hallowed home. When she arrived back home, the pictures had turned out dark and blurry. She had no real memory of being there. Not to worry, like a good husband, I escorted her back to Graceland a couple years later so she could really see Elvis's home.

The moral of this story, instead of snapping pictures on your cell phone just sit there and be mesmerized by where you are. For most people it's a once in a lifetime event. Don't spoil it.

We were fortunate to meet some old friends for lunch at the restaurant at Old Faithful Inn. There was grandmother, (our lifelong friend) her son and his four sons. The grandsons ranged in age from fourteen to twenty-four. They were polite boys who dutifully listened to our old peoples talk which is all we really ask as seniors.

To have a reunion, in this setting was a day to remember. The boys will soon be scattered to live their lives. One already had plans to teach in Spain in the fall.

The meal went quickly. It was time for them to leave. They were on the way to Cody, Wyoming. In our enjoyment of the day, we forgot to take any pictures. Oh well, only us sentimental oldies wanted that validation of the experience.

Interior of Old Faithful Inn.

GAY

It is sad that we do not use the word gay to describe our feelings or state of mind. Gay used to mean lite hearted and carefree. I miss the word gay. It has been removed from our everyday vocabulary.

Now gay refers to men who like men or women who like women. As Seinfeld says, "There is nothing wrong with that."

In the past, gays, usually hid their feelings from those around them. If, by accident, it was found out someone was gay, they were shunned and, in some cases, physically abused. We were afraid they would work some sort of mystic magic to change us to their persuasion.

Last summer in Yellowstone, I noticed that the gays were not ostracized. They were accepted into the group of young people. The gays did not advertise their leanings nor were they, "In the closet."

I worked with an openly gay young girl. She accepted who she was, so she was happy, vivacious and well adjusted. She had an open friendly way with our dining room customers and everybody else. One night she seemed pensive. I ask her, "What's up?" She replied, "I am having girl problems." I wasn't sure how to respond to her. I finally blurted out, "You know, you're an open honest person so hang in there and you will be fine." She gave me an eye to eye even steady look and said, "That's not bad for an old guy."

When I was young, I had a gay friend. I felt self-conscious around him because people might think that I was gay too. This was before, "Coming out of the closet" was fashionable. He moved around a lot. When he was in town, we would get together and talk. I am sad to say that he got depressed and did himself in. I feel that I should have done more for him. If he had lived in our society today, he might still be around.

There was a segment on 60 Minutes about a young girl swimmer that felt she was a boy. She was going to go to college at Harvard or Yale and she/he wanted to swim on the boy's team. The swim coach did not know how to handle this request. He called a team meeting. The boys on the swim team thought it was no big deal that she wanted to be a boy and swim with them. I say, "Good for them."

The Yellowstone crew that I worked with in The Grant Village Dining Room were awesome. They not only accepted gays as equals, but also workers from all over the world and an old man that was laboring to do his fair share. It was my privilege to be a part of a group like that.

What a great country we're becoming.

"POSTCARD FROM YELLOWSTONE"

Lower Falls of the Grand Canyon of the Yellowstone.

ZANDER

Zander was the bartender for the Seven Stool Saloon just off the lobby of the Grant Village Dining Room. He was a character and enjoyed joking around and kidding, so we hit it off right away. My Mother always told me, "kidding will get you in trouble." "Sorry, Ma."

Zander was in his upper twenties, long haired, and an Italian from Detroit. He had a perfect personality for his occupation, funny and a good conversationalist. He kept his seven stools and a few tables entertained.

About the third night on the job, he asked me how old I was. When I told him eighty-three, I thought I would have to pick him up off the floor. His mouth dropped open and he just stared at me. He probably thought that anyone in their eighties should be in assisted care. He must have blabbed to the rest of the dining room staff because they started treating me like a fragile heirloom. The treatment was nice for a while but once they got the idea that I could work and hold my own, they gradually started treating me as one of the gang. That was a nice feeling for me.

Zander carried bar glasses through the restaurant lobby to the kitchen for washing and carried the clean ones back. In the five hours the restaurant was open he made quite a few trips. One night, I was getting tired for him, making all those trips jetting back and forth so I said, "Zander, I think you are carrying the same glasses back and forth to show everyone how busy you are." He almost dropped the tray laughing. Zander and I enjoyed verbally sparring with each other. It made the evening work go quicker and made the job more fun.

One morning around 5:45am, I was taking off for work. I heard a guitar and singing coming from across the street where the smoking area was. It was Zander and two of his compadres. They had been up all-night drinking and having fun. I was envious. Oh, to be young again.

One night, in the middle of the night, Zander in a jubilant drinking mood must have crossed the line. He was fired by a security guard. I never heard the strait of it. Zanterra (The company we were employed by) was strict when you're out your out - clear out. In the time I was at Yellowstone many employees left either on their own or at the request of management. The departures were never explained. They were just gone. Sometimes we wouldn't notice for a week or so. If you would ask, the answer was always the same. A shrug of the shoulders or a blank look or sometimes a reply, "I dunno."

Zander slipped away in the night taking with him a part of my fun in Yellowstone.

THE VINTAGE YELLOW TOURING BUS

The Vintage Yellow Touring Bus

In the years 1935 to 1940 White Company out of Cleveland, Ohio, built close to one thousand touring vehicles for the Western National Parks. In 2006, Xanterra, won the contract to continue yellow bus tours. A company in Michigan refurbished seven of the yellow buses for $240,000 each. The buses now have around 135,000 miles on them.

I am a vintage car buff. Since arriving in The Park, the tour buses have fascinated me. The buses have three doors on one side and can hold 14 people.

The last week I was in Yellowstone, I decided to take a tour in one of these old vehicles that have been in the Park since the 1930s. I got up at 4:30am to drive from Grant Village up to Lake Hotel to catch the tour at 6:45am. The trip up to Lake was 23 miles. I met two cars on the winding road.

Guests have the first chance for the tours. If there are any seats left, the Xanterra employees could claim the seat free. Five guests had canceled that morning so there were just three of us. Two guests and me.

We had a driver/guide. I have forgotten his name so let's just call him Doug. Doug is a great name. One of the names not used for new male babies anymore. Sort of like the name Ronald.

Doug gave most of his attention to the paying guests. The tour was billed as a "Photographic tour." That way if we didn't see any wild animals, there would be no complaints.

The tour lasted for over four hours. Doug knew his stuff about the history of the Park, where the elk, moose and bears might to be. He also knew about cameras. The guest had an expensive camera and Doug helped him take some great pictures.

We saw three eagles roosting in a large tree. Doug said Yellowstone had one hundred Eagles. I thought there would be more. After all there is over two million acres in Yellowstone. Sixty miles by sixty miles. There are eighteen million acres in the Greater Yellowstone Ecosystem.

For me, the tour was a success. I got to ride in the yellow touring bus, saw some unbelievably gorgeous country and could make it back to Grant Village for an afternoon nap. Now that's living.

When we returned to the Lake Hotel, Doug took my picture in front of the yellow bus with the Lake Hotel in the background. Lake is the most upscale hotel in the Park. It reminds me of the Grand Hotel on Mackinac Island in Lake Michigan,

At the end of our tour and after the pictures were taken, I slipped Doug a twenty-dollar bill. That was cheap for all I saw and did. Doug's attitude toward me changed immediately. I was now his buddy. He was really an alright guy, just trying to eke out a living in one of the most beautiful areas in this country. I envied him.

Eagles roosting in a tree.

The author in front of the Lake Hotel.

HANNA

Hanna was one of our supervisors that worked in Grant Village Dining Room. Upon arrival in Yellowstone, we were inundated with meeting new fellow employees. It was difficult to remember all their names. I am terrible with names. I would forget my own name if I didn't get a letter occasionally.

As a trick to remember Hanna's name, we started calling her Hanna from Alabama. We never called her that to her face of course, she being the boss and all. We must have had an implanted spy in our staff because halfway through the summer she found out. The rhyme didn't bother her a bit. She said, "Last summer they called me Hanna from Montana."

The dining room staff always had a little meeting before our shifts. The meeting was conducted by one of our supervisors. She or he would inform us on where we needed to improve. Then the servers and assistant servers would be assigned a station in the dining room for that meal.

I did get scolded by Hanna a few times. One was for giving coffee away free. She put her hand on my shoulder, sister like, and said, "Ron you're not to give coffee away. The hand on the shoulder helped my ego but it is hard to be eighty-three and be reprimanded by a twenty some year old.

When business in the dining room got really hopping It was noisy and chaotic. The host was usually Annette because management wanted us seniors working together. Anyway, Annette would yell out the table number where I was supposed to seat the dinners. Due to my haste and bad hearing, sometimes the guests would end up being seated at the wrong table. This only happened when Hanna was around. When I returned to the host desk, she would give me the evil eye.

I enjoyed working in the dining room. It was exhilarating to be among the young staff and the pleasure of conversing with people from all over the world.

One evening when we were having pizza with our new friends, Tim and Annette, at the local drinking trough, Hanna and Justin came in together for a drink. Justin is one of the best servers in the dining room. He is a calm unflappable guy. When we were super busy and had a walk-in table of ten, I would in a panic run and find Justin. I would spout out, "Can you handle a table of ten?" He would always look at me calmly and say, "Sure, Ron." What a guy. Everybody liked him. On those rare times the servers were not busy, they would hang out with Justin in the corner of the dining room. I would wander over to hear what was going on. Justin would say, "Ron this is a servers meeting." I knew he was kidding me, but it was still hard to take the rejection.

Seeing Justin and Hanna together set the rumor mill a flutter for some time. We liked them both. Hanna and I had our issues, but she couldn't help being a boss.

The word around the dining room was that they wanted Justin to move up to management, but he declined. Good for him. We wanted him to stay as one of us.

To this day, I don't know if Hanna was from Alabama or Montana. She had a slight southern accent so I would lean towards Alabama.

I'M YOUR HUCKLEBERRY

It seems like everything out here in Yellowstone has huckleberries in it. Ice cream is where I first noticed it. It has a lite purple color with dark huckleberries throughout. The ice cream was delicious, and I ate it every chance I got.

The huckleberries grow wild here in the Northwest. It is said that you can't domestically grow them. I wonder with so many huckleberries being used, how growing in the wild would satisfy the demand. Having worked in Yellowstone for the summer, I have never heard someone say they used to work on a huckleberry farm.

I have heard that bears love huckleberries. Since I have made a great effort while working in Yellowstone to stay away from bear habitats, I will gladly take the word of those in the know about bear likes and dislikes.

The stores sell many products with huckleberries in them: jam, beer, barbecue sauce, ice cream, just to mention a few.

The term "I'm your huckleberry" was used in the 1993 movie "Tombstone." Val Kilmer played Doc Holiday, the gun fighter, dentist, gambler and drunk. Doc and Wyatt Earp were friends and fought together in the famous, "Gun fight at the O K corral" on October 6, 1881. Twice in the movie Doc or Val said, "I'm your huckleberry," when the nefarious Ringo was looking for a gun fight. I googled the term and it means, "I am the person for the job."

My wife and I brought many huckleberry products home to the Low Country of South Carolina. When they are gone, huckleberries will only be a memory of our summer in Yellowstone.

"POSTCARD FROM YELLOWSTONE"

Are you looking at me?

MONTANA

The studio of Charlie Russell.

While working in Yellowstone, my wife and I were given the same two days off a week. That way we could plan car trips around the area. Joyce has always had a fascination for Montana.

We had seen the movies, "Legends of the Fall" and "A River Runs Through It." Both movies were filmed in Montana and revealed some gorgeous country.

We decided to leave Grant Village after work on Friday and drive 139 miles to Bozeman, Montana, that evening. It was summer and the days were long, so we hoped to make it to Bozeman before it got dark. All the employees in Yellowstone knew just how many miles it was to the Walmart in Bozeman. Walmart represented civilization.

The trip to Bozeman took us out through West Yellowstone, a small tourist city just west of Yellowstone. The drive to West Yellowstone is slow because of tourist traffic and the somewhat narrow roads in Yellowstone. Next to the roads the terrain in Yellowstone is steep. The mountains and green conifer trees slope down to the roads. There are no wide-open spaces.

Once we started North from West Yellowstone on State Route 287, you are in Montana. The mountains are further from the highway creating wide green valleys. The country is wide open displaying beautiful scenery. A river even runs through some of the valleys as we head North.

Bozeman is a modern city of forty- five thousand. Located in a wide valley with mountains surrounding it. If you fly to Yellowstone, it is cheaper to fly into Bozeman than Jackson, Wyoming. The word on Jackson Hole, Wyoming, is that the billionaires have run the millionaires out.

After staying at a super Holiday Inn, we ate breakfast the next morning at a nice local eatery called, "The Western Cafe." The restaurant was filled with friendly local people. I must have been served a half a pound of hash brown potatoes. I didn't complain.

After breakfast, we toured the famous Walmart that everyone in Yellowstone talks about. We had a list from people back in Yellowstone to purchase items for them. On the buy list was three fly swatters. The mosquitoes around Lake Yellowstone are mean and hungry. Lake Yellowstone is large and very scenic, but it does have its drawbacks. The mosquitoes would be the big drawback.

The next stop on our adventure to Montana was Great Falls one hundred and eighty-three miles away. We arrived late in the afternoon just in time to visit the Charlie Russell Museum. The modern structure was a wonder to see. Many displays of Western culture and Charlie Russell paintings were hanging on the walls. The gift shop was especially large with items of all sorts for sale. Beside the Museum was the house Charlie Russell had lived in. Next to that was his large log building where he painted. The story goes that he used to paint in his house, but his wife kicked him out. She said there were to many paintings laying around.

Charlie was a cowboy before he became a painter. The way he incorporated action in his paintings was his trademark.

The three-structure complex was a privilege to visit. The place was clean, neat and the subject matter was fascinating.

The next morning, we drove out east of Great Falls to the Lewis and Clark Museum. The museum, like the Russell museum, was a modern building and was located right next to the Missouri River. You could look out the many big windows in the Museum and see the scenic Missouri River. I don't know how the Missouri River got clear up in Montana. I should have payed more attention to geography in school instead of writing notes to girls. The museum had many life like displays of Indian cultures, a boat the actual size used by Lewis and Clark and also early Montana settlers items.

I believe older people get more out of museums than kids do. I propose to stop taking school students on field trips to museums. It's such a waste. My idea is to pass a law that you must be over fifty to get into a good modern museum.

After visiting the Lewis and Clark Museum we headed the Honda south 315 miles to Yellowstone. The two and a half days we were traveling, we drove around 700 miles. Montana was all we expected it to be and more.

We would have to work another week before we got our two days off to hopefully take another trip around this great area.

We pulled into the parking lot of Grant Village. When we opened the door, we were attacked by an army of mosquitoes. Good thing we had three fly swatters. The old timers out here say that mosquitoes only last two weeks. They said that a month ago.

I am headed through the swinging doors for another evening of playing cards and chasing wild women with my old Buckaroo buddies Wish me luck!

TIM & ANNETTE

My reminiscing on the "Summer in Yellowstone" would not be complete without paying tribute to the wonderful couple we worked, traveled, ate, and loafed with during the memorable summer.

We met them on our first night in Yellowstone. They were with us when Tom guided us on the "Death March." If we had not had their generous friendship, our "Summer in Yellowstone" would not have been as much fun. We probably would have left Yellowstone much earlier.

Tim was a porter in the Housekeeping Department. Most older people would not have taken on the grueling, demanding tasks of a porter. Tim took his duties on as a challenge and with an enthusiastic smile. In fact, Tim used his own bicycle so he could complete his workload quicker.

Annette worked with me as a host in the Dining Room. She worked what was called, "The board." Being a host meant that she greeted all the customers with a smile and cheerfulness. She also answered the phone, posted reservations on the computer, assigned the customers to a certain table while making sure that each server (waiter/waitress) got an even number of tables. After all that she handed me the menus. I was called "The runner." I escorted the diners to their assigned table.

On the mornings Annette didn't work the early shift, she gladly provided coffee for me. They had brought from home a full-sized coffee maker, so she usually made a full pot of excellent coffee. Most of the time when I had a morning off, I slept in and missed breakfast and my precious coffee that I couldn't live without. I must have looked pathetic standing at her dorm door with my shaky hands clasping my empty coffee mug. She saved my coffee-less morning life on more than one occasion.

In the evening when all of us were off, we would meet in the second-floor lobby of the dorm and play cards or dominoes. Sometimes one of the younger groups would join us. They always added a fun element because they came from all over the world. A girl from Alaska would sit and watch us. The word was that she had a collection of knives. Most of the staff feared her so they stayed away and gave her a wide berth. We heard one morning in the E D R that she had been escorted out of the Park. We never saw her again.

When the four of us got the same day off, we would plan a car trip outside the Park. The first trip was to Cody, Wyoming, which was a hundred miles away. Cody is a town of around ten thousand people. The town felt to us like we were back in civilization. It had a Walmart and even a McDonalds. The Buffalo Bill museum was also in Cody. The first thing we were told when we arrived in Yellowstone, was that buffaloes are supposed to be called bison. So we were wondering if, to be correct, should the Museum be called Bison Bill Cody? The Museum is still called Buffalo Bill Cody, correct or not. We discovered that since we worked for Zanterra our admission was free. YEAH! The Museum was large and modern. There were many colorful Western history displays. They even had a live adult eagle. Buffalo Bill built a hotel and an ajoining Western dining room in downtown Cody. There was a long wooden bar with a huge mirror behind it. A unique chandelier made of Elk antlers hung in the dining room. Buffalo Bill gave the bar and dining room to his youngest daughter Irma, so, the place is called "Irma's." We had a wonderful prime rib buffet meal there for eleven bucks, senior rate of course.

We left Cody with full bellies and content in the fact that one hundred miles of beautiful county lies in front of us on the way back to Yellowstone. Tim drove so I gave him twenty dollars for gas. If I drove, he would give me a twenty. This went back and forth all summer. I'm not sure who ended up with the twenty but who cares because we all had a great time traveling through some heavenly scenic country.

The next adventure the four of us went on was a seventy-mile trip South to Jackson, Wyoming. Jackson Hole is the area, Jackson is the City. We visited a huge modern grocery store with much glee. It made us all a little homesick. Then we took in a western bar downtown across from the Antler City Park. They have saddles for stools at the bar upon which you can sit and have a drink. Most people only have one drink at the bar because the saddles are so uncomfortable. Western cowboy paraphernalia adorn the walls. On the wall downstairs by the rest rooms is something that should be in every bar in the Country. It was a breathalyzer to check for alcohol. If I remember right, it only cost fifty cents. Most drunks feel nothing is wrong. They are alright. They are just having a good time. I would propose that when a person comes into a bar, they give the bartender their vehicle keys just like the old West when they had to check their guns. The drinker would get his keys back only when he or she passed the breathalyzer test on the way out.

On the way out of town, we stopped at McDonalds for drinks to sip on the way back. It was a little bit of civilization that we yearned for in Yellowstone. The trip back to Yellowstone was enjoyable. The Grand Tetons were on our left as we motored North.

The last trip we took as a foursome was to Virginia City and Nevada City Montana. One of the young girls that worked with us in the Dining Room was from the area. She told us, "You have to go and see this area and towns." We drove to West Yellowstone then turned North into Montana. Montana is never disappointing. The drive revealed high distant mountains with large valleys between. Sometimes the panoramic views sweep clear to the distant horizon. It's all a Western paradise. The glorious view reminded me of the song, "We'll build a little nest, somewhere out in the West, and let the rest of the world go by.

Virginia City and Nevada city were old mining towns. The same old buildings are still standing. They are being used as commercial tourist stores. We rode the old train from Virginia City to Nevada City; about a mile. In Nevada City there was an historic museum. The man that started the museum traveled all of Montana buying old historic buildings. They were moved to Nevada City and set up like a little town. There was a jail, old barn, blacksmith shop, a shoes shop and many old residential wood structures. We did not have time to see it all. We felt grateful that someone with such farsightedness saved all those unique old buildings that showed us what Montana must have looked like in years past.

On the way back we saw an eagle sitting on a fence post. Back in Yellowstone, Tim knew about a small one lane, one-way road that snaked along the mountain side with an excellent view of the stream below. We came upon a spot where people came to swim. Looking down we could spot many swimmers perched on rocks and ledges like a flock of birds. Mountain streams are notoriously cold from the melted mountain snow. Most of the swimmers did not stay in the water long. Our vantage point looking down on the stream and the swimmers scattered about made the whole scene, a sight to behold.

Tim and Annette were an easy-going congenial couple. It was our joy and luck to spend our free time in Yellowstone with them. Our festive trips gave us something to look forward to which helped us make it through the long work weeks.

Annette, Tim, Ron and Joyce A happy foursome.

KARL WITH A "K"

When I first met Karl, a woman introduced him as Karl with a K. That introduction hounded Karl all summer. We all referred to him as Karl with a K.

Karl worked in the Registration Office. One of the elite positions in Grant Village. We all had uniforms when we worked. Karl and his compadres in registration wore a tie. A tie in Yellowstone is like a bikini at an AARP convention.

Most everybody that worked in Grant Village ate their meals at the E D R. (Employees Dining Room) This is where all the employees from House Keeping, Campgrounds, Lake House Restaurant, Grant Village Dining Room and Registration mingle. In the group Karl worked with, not many came to the E D R. Xanterra, the company we all worked for, charged one hundred and three dollars a week for room and board. Most of the tie wearers must have lived in campers. They were a frugal lot.

The food at the E D R was excellent. In fact, I looked up the supervisor of the kitchen and said, "I have a complaint about the food." She frowned, then replied, "What's your complaint?" "It's too good" I sternly said. "I wanted to lose ten pounds while here this summer." She smiled and walked away.

Karl with a K ate in the E D R and slept in the dorm. Just like the rest of us peons. Karl was from Columbus, Ohio, and said he was recruited by the illustrious Woody Hayes in 1968. Karl was a linebacker from South High School. We always had things to talk about since I am an avid Ohio State fan. Joyce calls me fanatical. In our wide-ranging conversations, he let it drop that he was an attorney. I thought attorneys never retired. With their last breath they would be hurrying to the courthouse to record a will or a deed before they kicked the bucket. He was here in Yellowstone alone. What happened to his wife? Did she run off with his law partner? Was he in witness protection for squealing on "THE MOB?" An undisciplined mind can roam without restraint.

Karl with a K, working in the Registration Office of Grant Village was privy to information us work-a-day commoners were not aware of. He informed me how to catch a free ride on one of those vintage yellow touring buses that I was so fascinated with.

Although Karl smoked little stogies, he was in good condition. He went on hikes in the Park. He even did the full moon hike up Mount Washburn.

Karl was part of the glorious group that met in the lobby of the dorm on our nights off. He was usually reading but he would converse with any and every one that wanted to talk. The cute, giggly girls from Thailand would be sitting around talking in their native tongue. Lee, our big, good natured, articulate Navajo Indian buddy from Arizona was observing the goings on from the corner. Billiard balls were banging on the pool table, while the foosball group were noisily shouting and from the weight room, we could hear the weights clanging and the exercisers grunting. The ping pong ball made their own unique sound as they were slammed across the wood table. The whole group was a happy lot that made you feel good to be a part of. Us oldies played dominoes or cards until our curfew. The younger set doesn't seem to worry about a good night's sleep. The festivities were to end at eleven so all of us could get a good night's sleep. In the morning we would all be bright and peppy so we can give our all for Zanteera and Yellowstone.

Forgive me, I have gotten way away from my new buddy Karl. He was just one of the many memorable people that I met while in Yellowstone. I might look him up if I ever get back to old "Columbus town." It is hard to find someone now. It used to be that all you had to do was look in the phone book and get his number and address. Now everyone has unlisted cell phones and no land lines. I could look up his name on land deeds at the courthouse or by computer if I knew how. Sorry Karl, it would have been fun to chat with you about our memories of Yellowstone and OHIO STATE FOOTBALL.

MARIETTA HIGH SCHOOL

A spunky young girl has joined our diverse crew of hosts in the Grand Village Dining Room. She is medium height, dark hair with white tips and a complexion like Halle Berry. She is pleasant, outgoing and fun to be around. Being young she mastered the job immediately. I am still learning to cope.

One morning an older gentleman with a Marietta High School sweatshirt on came wandering into the dining room. The new host spotted the sweatshirt. She gave the gentleman a dazzling smile and said, "Marietta High School in Georgia, I used to go there." The guy smiled back and said, "Class of 1966." Our host said, Class of 2016."

There was an immediate genuine connection. The gentleman's wife snapped a picture of the two of them smiling proudly into the camera.

Observing this, I thought how different the times were, 1966-2016. There have been some huge social changes in fifty years. Back in 1966 the South was in turmoil, a war really. The Civil Rights Movement, the lunch counter sit-ins, the boycott of city buses, and trying to register black voters. I will bet back in 1966 there were no black students in Marietta High School.

For an old liberal, seeing this display of friendship of these two from different generations and races brought a lump to my throat.

Just maybe this old country of ours is going to turn out alright after all.

PHANTOM IN THE BASEMENT

Under the Grant Village Dining Room and kitchen Is a cavernous basement. The employees are required to dash down there for supplies. We are always in a hurry because that's the expected pace for the dining room and kitchen staff.

To go down in that vast underground basement is both bewildering and scary. We are not sure where the item is that we're looking for and we are alone in that huge area. The atmosphere is quiet and spooky.

As we rummage through the shelves and boxes hoping to stumble onto what we are looking for, a male voice comes from right behind us, "Can I help you?"

The first thing you do is jump. Next you try to recapture your breath and settle the heart. You utter what you were sent down for. He seems to always know where the item is that you want. You grab your item that's needed and immediately take flight. You say your thanks and head for the stairs.

The rumor has floated around the restaurant that the mysterious man might live down there. Not unlike the Phantom of the Opera. He has approached most of us in the same manner. We thought we were alone down there but, "boom," there he is right behind us.

I, being the oldest of all the help in the kitchen and dining room, decided to take it upon myself to put the rumors to rest and befriend, "The Phantom." Come to find out his name is Tony. The reason he knows where everything is down there is because he works there. That's his job.

Tony and I became on "speaking terms," even friendly. "This could be the beginning of a beautiful relationship." The last line in the movie Casablanca.

If he would just stop appearing behind us. Maybe we could supply him with some heel plates. Do you know what heel plates are? Back in, "the day," we would put these little steel plates on the back of the heels of our shoes so the heels would last longer. They would click walking down the sidewalk or down the marble halls at school. Sort of like a tap dancer. It sounded cool so those of us that had heel plates felt cool and everybody knew when we were coming. Now a days everyone wears tennis shoes. The kids call them sneakers. Heel plates don't fit on sneakers.

I have lost the thread of this story. Tony was good at his job. He knew where everything was. He scared the bejeebies out of us, but we survived. Life goes on.

JOHN & KAY
THE GOOD LIFE

One morning, I was hanging around the host's station waiting for breakfast customers to appear and trying to look busy.

A couple in their early thirties walked in and started to look at the photographs on the wall. There were eight photographs of Yellowstone in various seasons and locations. The pictures were good, and many guests had admired them.

As usually, I walked up and struck up a conversation. I inherited this gift from my sainted mother. Bless her heart.

The couple's names were John and Kay. John had worked in this dining room as a bartender in 1999. He had taken all the pictures on the wall. He was surprised and pleased that the photographs were still on display. Kay had worked in Yellowstone in 2003. They met and have been together ever since.

They now live in Montana. John is a cook and Kay is a server. They work 4:00am till 10:00am every day during the busy season. They have three big dogs which are their pride and joy. The dogs get along well and they take them everywhere they go. Even to work.

John told me about his beloved Montana. They live near Bozeman. He recommended that I should see Virginia City, Montana and eat in Ennis, Montana.

He also informed me that the Forrest Service has primitive cabins all over Montana that rent for $45.00 a night. They had rented one near Bozeman in the mountains.

Sitting around their campfire they could watch the lights of Bozeman come on in the evening.

From John and Kay's enthusiastic conversation you could feel their enjoyment of where they lived and the unique lifestyle they had created for themselves. In these eight to five worlds of ours, stumbling on this happy couple was a treat. They heard a different drummer and I, for one, am a little envious.

I picture where they live as a small place up a winding mountain road. There would be a few stacks of firewood waiting for the winter weather. A front porch so they can watch the sun set, and a four-wheel drive, four door pickup truck parked in the front yard. They would have four doors so they can have a seat for the dogs.

All of us, at one time or another have wanted to step away. It was great to meet a couple who had done it and it worked for them.

Meeting John and Kay was one of the highlights of my summer in Yellowstone.

BEARTOOTH HIGHWAY

If you are fortunate enough to visit Yellowstone, you must take a day drive on The Beartooth Highway. US 212. The road traverses through the Northeast entrance of Yellowstone. You will travel through Lamar Valley where all kinds of wild animals can be spotted.

Charles Kuralt the host of CBS's "On the Road" called this stretch of highway, "The most beautiful road in America."

Beartooth is loaded with what I call, "Shut my mouth" type scenery. I say this because your mouth is always hanging open at the panoramic views.

The day we drove Beartooth Highway there were many motorcycles touring the same area. It was a week before the big bike rally at Sturgis, South Dakota. Most of the Bikers were older and did not fit the image Marlon Brando portrayed in the 1953 movie, "The Wild One." Motorcycles are expensive so it takes an older affluent person to afford the hobby.

We drove over the 10,947-foot pass called, "Dead Indian Pass." At the top was a parking area where a paved hiking path guided us to a high overlook. We had a spectacular view of the mountains and valleys we had just passed through and the country yet to come.

At the lookout point, fat little chip munks came begging for food. If you had sunflower seeds or bird seed, they would eat out of your hand. Even old stale cookies would do the trick. We hadn't brought along any food. Once they found out we were foodless, we were dropped from there, "Let's be friends" list.

This enchanting trip took us to Cook City, Red lodge and back around to Cody, Wyoming. In Cody we stopped at Irma's. The old Western dining room and bar was the perfect place to top off our day.

After a delicious meal in a place built by Buffalo Bill, we drove the hundred miles back to our room in Yellowstone. As we watched the gorgeous mountain scenery pass outside our car windows, we couldn't help but wonder about the people that had settled this area and the hardships they endured through. Now we pass in an air condition car in a tenth of the time it took them with horse and wagon.

We arrived back at Grant Village having driven a three-hundred mile circle knowing we would never forget this day on Beartooth Highway.

"POSTCARD FROM YELLOWSTONE"

The air out here in Yellowstone is so pure and clear that I can almost see heaven. I am enjoying the view because it is the closest I may ever get.

RONDA

One of the things from home that I missed while in Yellowstone was Ronda. Don't jump to conclusions. Ronda is my bright red Ford Ranger pickup truck with a stretch cab. There are two jump seats back of the front seat. These seats are for little people or small children, but my tall, skinny 16-year-old grandson somehow can squeeze himself in on one of the back seats.

For some time now I have named my vehicles. This naming promotes them to family status. My last car was a 1992 Chrysler La Baron convertible called, "The Red Baron." I owned the car for seventeen years. As the years went by the Red Baron kept getting smaller. Thus, getting in and out became more physically challenging. Some commented that the difficulty was due to the age of the owner. I prefer to think that the car shrunk. If I had kept the convertible any longer, it would have become toy size. The Red Baron was given to my perfect grandson because I can't deny him a thing.

Naming my new pickup was not easy. My first choice was, "The Red Ryder." For those of you who are too young to remember the great comic book era, Red Ryder along with Little Beaver, his side kick, were comic book heroes who helped bring law and order to the old West. Many of the comic book heroes were repopularized by block buster movies. Superman, Batman, Lone Ranger, and Spider-man just to name a few. Red Ryder did not make the leap from comic books to the big screen. There are very few serious comic book readers still left from my generation that would remember Red Ryder and Little Beaver. To me, they still deserve to take their rightful position among our comic book legends of the past.

After driving Red Ryder about a month, I became painfully aware that my precious pickup was female not male. A man can tell. What was I to do?

I remember the beautiful red headed women from the past: Lucile Ball, Ronda Fleming, Rita Hayworth. Although Ronda was a knockout, I have issues with naming sons junior. The name Ron and Ronda could be construed as a junior. Women never name their daughters after themselves. Why is that? After much consternation, the pickup was christened Ronda. After all, I do know a couple of juniors that turned out to be tolerable. Plus, Ronda had those flirty, "Let's have fun eyes."

Ronda is not perfect. She has a dinged-up windshield. The back bumper is banged up some. She is a little sluggish on the take off. I must manually crank the windows up and down and she visits the mechanic with some regularity. All this doesn't bother me because I am a little dinged up, slower than I used to be and often must visit the doctor.

Harper Lee got a new watch in her later years. She said, "This will see me through." I was saddened when I first read this comment. Now that I am in my eighties, I believe that Ronda will see me through. Now Harper's wise comment gives me a certain comfort and peace.

It is altogether fitting that my first car was a 1937 Ford. I bought the car for $40.00. It was fifteen years old when I purchased it. I bought the 2001 Ford Ranger in 2017 for $5,000.00. The truck was sixteen years old when purchased.

There is some sort of simile in that, but it alludes me.

STONERS

Tom, our training instructor, upon our arrival in Yellowstone (remember he was the guide on the "Death March") warned us, "Be careful, Yellowstone can bite you." His inference was that we had come to one of the most beautiful, scenic, pristine, unpopulated areas in the lower forty-eight States. You're in-God's country. What can all those people that swarm around the big cities be thinking? How could they be happy with all the noise, dehumanizing traffic, smog, fumes and crowds?

When you start thinking like that, you have been badly bitten by Yellowstone. You may be able to slip away for the winter or a family visit, but Yellowstone will always be calling you back. It's a pull you can't resist.

You are only comfortable among the mountains, rivers and the quiet, peaceful solitude of the special place called Yellowstone.

I have met people who live in the area and work in Yellowstone. They came to work for the summer, ten, twenty, even thirty years ago and never left. Once you have stayed that long, there is no going back. You're a Yellow stoner, or I just call them, "Stoners." I respect, even envy the "Stoners." The life they lead is hard but the country they live in makes up for the sacrifices.

It could be, if I was younger and had a comfortable log cabin up an old mountain road, a large stack of firewood for the winter and a luxurious four-wheel pickup truck, I might be persuaded to live the good life. After eighty-three years of living so close to everything I would feel isolated and lonely. There would be no Whoppers, bagels, libraries or card games which are the lifeblood of my existence.

Years ago, in my youth, a friend and I worked in Sun Valley, Idaho. We rode motorcycles in the beautiful, rugged Sawtooth Mountain Range. We worked and played in Idaho on and off for nearly six years. We eventually migrated back to Ohio to live our lives and although we were fortunate to have wonderful wives and loving families, we still longed to be back among those mountains of Idaho.

My lifelong friend is gone now. We can no longer reminisce about our grand old days in Idaho. I hope the modern-day "Stoners" appreciate fully their unique existence in an area few people get to see, let alone live there.

AL

Grant Village had various departments. There was Grant Village Dining Room, where I worked, Lake House Restaurant, Housekeeping, Camping, and Reservations. Each of the Departments had a supervisor. Most of them were decent people but a few suffered from being promoted to their position of incompetence.

Al was the big Kahuna of all of Grant Village. It took me a while to figure this out. Al would show up all over the place in his western boots, vest and a black cowboy hat with a braided ponytail hanging down his back. This whole western image went over well with the guests. He was soft spoken and never seemed to give any orders. Some of the staff and especially the supervisors got uptight when he moseyed around. He just seemed to be checking things out. It got so I even began to get jumpy when he dropped by unannounced.

I admired the way he dressed and handled himself. I enjoyed wearing my western clothes when in the West. Wanting to dress like a cowboy goes back to my youth. In the early to late Forties, the Strand Theater in Delaware, Ohio, showed two western movies every Saturday afternoon. Cowboys were my heroes. Willie Nelson got it right when he sang;

> "I grew up a dreamin
> Of being a cowboy
> Lovin the cowboy ways
> Pursuing a life
> Of my high riding heroes
> I burnt up my childhood days"

Even today, in my eighties, I enjoy wearing my western duds and emulating my western heroes that I idolized so much as a kid.

I admired Al, his image, the quiet way he approached his job. He was the perfect fit to be the ramrod of Grant Village.

"POSTCARD FROM YELLOWSTONE"

Lewis Falls on the way the Jackson Hole.

THE GEYSERS OF YELLOWSTONE

Yellowstone has sixty percent of the world's geysers. Old faithful, the iconic symbol of Yellowstone, is the most famous geyser. In our morning adventure jaunts around Yellowstone, we would spot the white puffs of steam above the geysers silhouetted against the blue morning sky. A thing of beauty to be remembered. This panoramic scene reminded us of how lucky we were to be in Yellowstone.

Geysers are low on my totem pole of things to see and do in Yellowstone. Seeing hot water boil out of the earth doesn't do much for me. There are geyser enthusiasts, who get up early in the morning to visit the geysers before the crowds. I wish them well. They sure came to the right place.

Legend has it that fisherman would catch trout from Lake Yellowstone, then dip the fish in one of the hot springs to cook them. There was also the rumor that a Ranger came upon a man trying to squeeze a bear into the front seat of his car to get a good picture. Another rumor has it that a man tried to lift his son onto the back of a Bison. Like Ripley said, "Believe or not."

Tourists in Yellowstone do mysterious acts of ignorance. I have seen a tourist when they have spotted a wild animal stop their car even if it's in the middle of the road and take off running towards the wild creature.

A man was arrested in Yellowstone for taunting a bison in the middle of the road. He was found in another state and arrested. After all, this land is theirs, we are the invaders. The animals always have the right of way in Yellowstone.

Let me preach just for a bit. A lot of people feel that the earth is here just for them. They indiscriminately dam the free-flowing rivers, cut the trees, destroy the mountains to get their precious minerals, pollute the air and dump whatever they don't want in the ocean. We are sure creating a "wonderful" legacy for our grandchildren and great grandchildren. I apologize for my ranting but that's what old men do.

But I digress from the unique geysers of Yellowstone. Yellowstone has so much to offer. We were there for a summer and still didn't get to see it all. If we ever return, the beautiful geysers in the early morning would be at the top of our list. Most tourist visit the Park an average of two days. They see an elk, bison or maybe a bear if they are lucky. They take in Old Faithful then split for another National Park like The Black Hills of South Dakota.

That's alright because other tourists keep coming into the Park. We quit going to the sites of Yellowstone in July because the tourist haunts were too crowded. If I was to return to Yellowstone, it would be in September. The kids have gone back to school, and the parents are saving for their next vacation. September could be cold and sometimes snowy, but you would not have to fight the crowds and traffic.

The picturesque geysers would still be there as they have been for hundreds of years. Hopefully they will never change.

THE YELLOW STONE

One morning I was cleaning the window smudges on the front door of the dining room. A task that was my job to do at the end of each shift. See you thought it was all just a summer of fun and games.

A woman was standing there so we started talking. In the West people and just more open and friendly. It was easy to start a communication. You begin with, "Where you from," or "What are you going to see in Yellowstone today?"

She told me that she had worked in Yellowstone the summer of 1982. I will save you the math. If she was twenty in 1982 that would make her fifty-six. She rode the Greyhound bus here from Miami, Florida. For some reason her luggage ended up in San Francisco. She was issued two uniforms for work. She slept in one and worked in the other. I did not ask about the other clothing. Some things men just don't want to know. The luggage showed up two weeks later.

She was here with her now fiancé. He had worked here in Yellowstone that same summer so many years ago. They had stayed in contact over the years through her three marriages and three divorcees.

She had moved from Miami to Chattanooga seven years ago. I am not sure how long they have been together. Now they are on a sentimental journey back to Yellowstone where they first met.

Upon arrival, he had presented her with an engagement ring. The ring had two stones, one was her birth stone and the other was a yellow stone. She glowed as she related her story to me. Then she showed me her beautiful ring.

He appeared out of the men's room. They were both flushed with their new relationship. It was a joy to see.

They had weathered the ups, downs, twists and turns that life's road takes us. Now they were in Yellowstone for a new beginning.

I wished them good luck but somehow, I don't think they will need it.

HOMEWARD BOUND

In the first week of August, we made the decision to bring our summer adventure in Yellowstone to a close. We had seen the scenic sites of the area and the work grind was taking its toll. Our life in South Carolina was calling us back.

On August 9th, we arose at 6:00am, washed and dried our bed sheets and two sets of uniforms. Our room was inspected for cleanliness and damage. We turned in our clean sheets, uniforms and badges. The badges had our name and where we were from printed on them. I was hoping to save them as a keep sake.

All the checking out duties delayed our departure until noon. Now I understood why the other deserters escaped in the middle of the night.

There was no sadness as we drove away. We had seen Yellowstone in all its splendor. We were ready to say goodbye. Our "Summer in Yellowstone," the people we met and the scenery we viewed will always be a joy to remember.

CHEYENNE

The first stop on our odyssey back to South Carolina after our work/vacation summer in Yellowstone is Cheyenne.

No Western trip is complete without a stopover in Cheyenne, Wyoming. Just the name Cheyenne conjures up, in our minds, visions of noble Indians in their war paint and their colorful outfits sitting bareback on pinto ponies.

Cheyenne is the crossroad of the West. The Cross-Continental Railroad reached Cheyenne in 1867 on its rush to connect with the railroad coming from Sacramento, California. The two railroads met in Utah at Promontory Point on May 10, 1869. This made it possible to ride the train from New York City to Sacramento, California. Our young country was at last had an East/West connection.

In the old days Cheyenne was the jumping off place for the gold seekers setting out for the Black Hills of South Dakota. Wild Bill Hickok was one of the hoards heading North from Cheyenne to get rich in the gold fields around Deadwood.

I had been through Cheyenne many times on the Union Pacific Railroad in the 1950's. I worked at Sun Valley, Idaho which was owned by Union Pacific Railroad. They provided their employees with a free train pass home. I would board the train in Shoshone, Idaho, a small town in the open prairie of southern Idaho. Thirty-six hours later, the train arrived in the loop of busy downtown Chicago. The experience from the open prairie to a major city in a short time was a huge adjustment.

On the way back West, I rode the Greyhound bus to Chicago. The bus pulled in at 11:30pm and the bus for Omaha left at 11:30pm. I was aware of this timely exchange, so I ran from one bus to catch the other. I was successful but my checked luggage was not so speedy. Usually it took a week for my suitcase to catch up to me at Sun Valley, Idaho.

But I digress, Wyoming was the first state to give women the right to vote in 1869. On the grounds of the State Capital Building in Cheyenne stands a statute of Esther Hobart Morris. She was the first woman in the United States to be a Justice of the Peace.

One shouldn't visit Cheyenne without touring the restored train station. I had passed through this station some sixty years ago not having any idea of its significance. On the corner next to the train station is a large western clothing store. On our trips through Cheyenne, I must always purchase something western. This piece of clothing will probably spend a lot of time hibernating in my closet. But I must have it. The last time through Cheyenne, I bought a western white shirt with snaps instead of buttons. I am not sure why the cowboys needed snaps, could be they were for when the cowboys visited ladies of the evening. In their haste, they could tug on the shirt and all the snaps would pop open quickly. It's just a theory. This time, I could not leave without buying a blue denim jean jacket.

As we drove South out of Cheyenne towards Denver the next day, I proudly wore my new blue denim jacket. The temperature outside the Honda was in the eighties but some of us sacrifice a little comfort for style.

TAOS

With the image of Cheyenne in our rear-view mirror, we motored down Inter-State 25 through Denver to our destination; Taos, New Mexico. New Mexico is known as the "Land of enchantment," which we found to be true. I have two cousins that live in Taos and their hospitality door is always open. Cousins Sara and Sue have retired in Taos. They have found refuge in this Western country with it's people and the way of life that exists here.

Taos is a town in Northeast New Mexico around seventy miles from Santé Fe. The town is surrounded by mountains and has a predominate southwestern/adobe atmosphere. Native Americans (Navajos) have lived in the area for centuries. Coronado trooped through the area in 1508 looking for gold. The Spanish stole the land from the Indians. After the United States/Mexican war of 1845, the Americans came to New Mexico and stole the land from the Spanish.

Around the 1920s, an artist/painter named Georgia O'Keeffe began her trips to Taos. Her presence started an artist colony that still exists today. In the 1970s the area became, "Hippyville." Actor Dennis Hopper is buried here and so is Kit Carson.

Cousin Sara built a traditional adobe casita or home. She acted as the general contractor and used Mexican laborers when possible. The casita is a traditional adobe dwelling. A Kiva fireplace is featured in the corner of her living room. The whole structure is a monument to Cousin Sara's dedication, stick-to-itiveness and hard work. She singularly willed this historic architecture home into existence.

To steal a glimpse of the real people of Taos, you must go to the local health food store. The true women of Taos show up with no makeup, long slightly gray hair and they look you in the eye when talking. Their vehicle of choice is usually a pickup truck. The men appear in jeans, flannel shirts and well-worn work boots. Their choice of ride is anything with four-wheel drive. The conversation in the store and parking lot is open and friendly.

There is a giant bulletin board on the entry wall of the health food store. The board advertises all kind of work for hire, cultural events, homes for sale, rooms for rent, wood for sale and much more. It's like the town center of communication.

The health food store has a buffet in the front part of the store. You can take out or have lunch there at one of the tables provided. In short, no trip to Taos is complete without a visit to the health food store.

On one of our trips to Taos, cousin Sue drove us to Walmart, the back way. We did not go by the Kit Carson home or his grave. We did not see the town square which is three hundred years old. We flew down old dusty roads. I think we might have cut through a few back yards before finally emerging in the back-parking lot at Walmart. Sue has opened our eyes. We would never think of Taos in quite the same way again. She should give tours.

Taos is the only place that I can wear my western get up and not feel out of place. The Taoists, Taosonians, Dudes or even Dames, whatever they refer to themselves as in this modern age of equality. Taos is a City of rugged individualists in one of the last environments for true self-expression without being judged. Women are not called dames anymore. They sacrificed that when the women movement came along, plus they lost their aprons and their claim of frailness. Not a bad trade.

Albuquerque hosts a colorful balloon festival in the first part of October. We were six weeks early. We were sure that cousin Sara's open-door policy did not extend to six weeks. Anyway, we were getting anxious to get back to our more normal routine of lazy retirement in South Carolina.

The Casita

Kiva fireplace

AFTER YELLOWSTONE

During the "Summer in Yellowstone," there was no television or newspapers. Before we left for the Park, when 6:30pm arrived everything came to a stop. I planted myself in front of the television for the evening news. I discovered while in Yellowstone that the world could get along very well without my watchful eye. That's a sad thing to discover. Years ago Huntley/Brinkley, my two favorite newscasters on National Broadcasting Company, retired which set me adrift for a believable television news channel. Cronkite was alright but he was too authoritarian for me. I did like the way he said, "And that's the way it was on September 6th, 1966, or whatever day. Edward R. Morrow was good too, but he smoked too much. It finally got him.

The newscasters today are too young to fathom the panoramic history of today's news. Upon my return to South Carolina, I have successfully given up, "The News."

The first thing I was going to do upon my arrival home was to stay in my pajamas for three days. I visioned ensconcing myself in the Lazy Boy and binging on television. I would start with watching all the Ohio State football games from the past year. On Netflix, I found the complete reruns of "Breaking Bad." It was filmed in Albuquerque, New Mexico. The same state where my cousins live. I could identify with the area and that was reason enough to watch the program. There were seventy-two episodes, each of them about an hour long. A perfect binge. Plus, the characters and the plot were captivating.

When out on an adventure, like we were on in Yellowstone, you dream of being home in the Lazy Boy. When you are comfortable in the easy chair at home, you dream of being on an adventure. Such is life.

As the days drift slowly by, and the number of days increase since we left Yellowstone, my mind increasingly revisits the memory of that special place. When I hear someone say "Yellowstone," I have been there. I have seen the places. Now I realize how precious those days were.

When people ask me how was Yellowstone. I try to be truthful and say, "It was a great time, but I would never do it again." They smile knowingly and think, "He wouldn't go back, why should I go way out there?" But really, I have been there, seen that and now hopefully I can move on to another new experience.

Tom said in one of his heart to hearts during our training sessions, "Watch out, Yellowstone will bite you. When spring breaks from winter, Yellowstone starts coaxing you back."

I would be honored to be a "Stoner" along with:

Doug, the yellow tour bus driver,

Tony, the phantom in the basement,

John & Kay, the couple from Montana that were living the good life,

Shirley & Bob, the couple from Florida that did eight consecutive summers in Yellowstone,

Al, who migrated from Iowa and never went back

Tom, our trainer and leader on the Death March,

Tyler is on my list of "Stoners" but he doesn't know he is a "stoner" yet.

ROUND-A-BOUTS

Round-a-bouts are designed so that traffic does not have to stop as it flows through an intersection. The theory is that without a traffic light, long lines of traffic are reduced going through an intersection.

These new modern round-a-bouts are traumatic for me to use. Bluffton, South Carolina, where I reside, has one of these circles of suicide. There are more but I only must use this one. The one I use is on the way to the library and the doctor's office. Two major thoroughfares converge on this round-a -bout.

I begin tensing up a block or so away from this traffic hazard. By the time I arrive, I am in full panic mode. Heavy traffic is flowing into this two-lane circle from four sides. My goal is to enter this maze, go past the first exit and take the second exit which means I am going straight. I am staying on the very same street I started on. If I accomplish this feat of vehicular dexterity without an irate motorist beeping his horn at me, it's a miracle.

As a senior in good standing, situations that bug me are increasing exponentially. Waiting in a doctor's office for thirty minutes bugs me, new cell phones that won't mind bugs me, a small kid crying loudly in a restaurant bugs me, watching some lunatic cut in and out in traffic at dangerous speeds bugs me and most of all people who are not disabled who park in a disabled parking space.

Personally, I think that round-a bouts should be banned from the face of the earth. If you agree, write your congressperson. Those congresspersons in office should have plenty of time to read your letter because they don't seem to be doing anything else of value with their time.

ROMAN HOLIDAY

Way back in the 1950's an appealing movie came out called "Roman Holiday." The movie starred Audrey Hepburn, (WOW) Gregory Peck and Eddie Albert. The movie was filmed in Rome which enhanced the pleasure of viewing the film with the beautiful buildings of Rome in the background.

The three stars drove around Rome in this little Fiat called "Cinque Cento" which means the little five hundred in Italian. I am a car buff, The Fiat impressed me with its smallness and the simplicity of getting around in this attractive little car. In the 1950's in the United States we were building these huge cars that had big motors, chrome bumpers and weighed around four thousand pounds. These monster cars were very roomy which included the back seat where there was enough room for a girl to get pregnant and many did. We boys must have had something to do with that even though it was always the girl's fault.

I enjoy looking at these vintage cars. They remind me of my youth. I knew guys that owned cars just like these. In fact, I was privileged enough to ride in them. Some guys look at women longingly, some get a rush holding a gun in their hands, me I like viewing old cars and women too for that matter. These 1950s automobiles had the public mesmerized over the status of owning one of these super vehicles. We knew that if we owned one of these shiny cars, we were really making it as a person and our life finally amounted to something.

Now back to the beautiful Audrey Hepburn and the Cinque Cento. I felt that little car was all you really needed to live the simple uncomplicated existence. Who needs all those big cars? I can picture myself riding along in this Fiat, no bills, no responsibilities, nor worries, just living the good life. Me and Audrey Hepburn.

Now fast forward sixty years, we were taking the grandchildren back to their parents. We had entertained them for almost three weeks, and they had to go back to school. Kids start to school the middle of August now. In my day we started school the first Tuesday after the first Monday in September. It was the American way. Anyway, our loaded to the hilt minivan pulled into one of these super-duper service plazas and what to my wondering eyes should appear but one of the newly designed Fiats that had a resemblance to the Fiat in Roman Holiday.

There it was in all its splendor a brilliant yellow and the same simple beautiful lines I remembered. I immediately went into a wonderful reverie of me and Audrey riding along through the countryside. She turns and bestows on me one of those 500 kilowatt smiles. I am not sure what happened to Gregory Peck or Eddie Albert in this dream but who cares, Audrey is here. I jolt myself back into reality. There is a man about my age driving the new Fiat. He is a little heavy, so he fills the driver's seat and his face also fills inside the windshield. I give him the thumbs up and point to the car of my dreams. He rolls down the window, puts his head out and shouts, "I hate it. I picked this car up in Dayton and I can't wait to return it."

My dream is shattered. No Roman Holiday for me. The beautiful Audrey is gone. Reality has set back in. Grandmother and the perfect grandchildren are back in my reality check. Oh well, the dream was fun while it lasted but I am still captivated by the vintage Fiat in Roman Holiday and the simplicity of the new Fiat.

SPITTING

I never knew either of my grandfathers. The only thing I have to go by are the stories my Aunts and Uncles shared with me. I was told that my grandfather Owens, a Welshman on my mother's side was a great spitter. Now that's not a good place to begin but it's all I have.

Back then, it was common for a man to chew tobacco. The men took pride in how far they could spit and how accurate they were. The men would sit around the stove in the old country store. The wood/coal stove was in the center of the store. The stove pipe ran the length of the store before it was vented outside. The long stove pipe could dispense heat all through the store. This was more efficient than venting the pipe straight up to the roof from the stove. The men would sit and talk and spit. When the spit hit the hot stove, it made a sizzle sound which pleases the spitter. The men sat and talked about the crops, weather and the latest gossip. One of the stories went like this: A farmer went to Florida for vacation. When he returned his silo was half empty. He went in and told the local Sheriff. The Sheriff ask him if he had told anyone. The farmer replied, "No." The Sheriff told him to go on home and not tell anyone even his wife. "If anyone asks you about the stolen corn bring his name to me." The farmer was sitting around the store one day chewing and spiting when the man next to him asked, "Did you ever find who stole your corn?" The farmer took the man's name into the Sheriff. The Sheriff went out and talked with the man and he confessed. Now that's good old time sheriffing.

In the old days there were spittoons everywhere. Most bars had spittoons on the floor next to the bar in hopes that the men didn't spit on the floor.

When I was sixteen and working on the highway road crew for the summer, I decided what was good enough for grandpa was good enough for me. I bought a plug of Brown Mule plug chewing tobacco and commenced to carry on the family tradition. Before long I began to get a wee bit dizzy. My stomach was doing flip flops. I even broke out in a sweat. Things worsened so I vowed, "Dear Lord, if you keep me from throwing up, I will never chew again." I didn't throw up and I never chewed again.

I know that all this chewing and spitting may sound gross to you. When it's compared against today's putting needles in your arms or snorting white stuff up your nose, a good old fashion chew doesn't seem that bad.

I LIKE IKE

Dwight David Eisenhower came to Delaware, Ohio in the Fall of 1951. He was running for President of the United States and was making a whistle train stop tour through Ohio. Harry Truman had successfully used the train in his campaign for the Presidency in 1947.

Ike was very popular. He was a top general in World War ll. Many of the young men who were voting age had served under Ike in Europe. Ike had a big winning smile and he was liked and respected by all, especially the Republicans whose ticket he was running on. Ike had beat Robert Taft of Ohio in the primary election to get the Republican nomination. The Republicans had been out of office of President since Roosevelt was elected in 1932.

We were let out of school so we could walk the eight blocks across town to the East side railroad tracks. We hurried down the street in mass. There were six grades of us. At least five hundred kids scurrying over to see Ike. In today's world, that would be a parent's and teacher's nightmare.

Delaware and Delaware County was ninety seven percent Republican at that time. The powers in control let us out of school. If Adlai Stevens, the Democrat running for President, had come to Delaware, we might have stayed in school. So, we liked Ike.

He made a speech. I can't remember what he said but he smiled and waved his hand. It was a great honor having him, a nominee for President in our hometown. I am writing this sixty-eight years later, so you understand the impression this whistle stop made on me.

In that era, Ohio Wesleyan University freshman always had to wear a red beanie. If the freshman was found without his red beanie, I would hate to speculate on the trouble he or she would be in. A beanie was ripped off a freshman's head and tossed up to Ike who put it on and displayed his dazzling smile.

After the goings on were over and the train pulled out, we must have spent all our energy because the trip back across town to school went painfully slow. It was said some never made it back.

Ike became President in 1952 replacing Harry Truman. John Kennedy was elected President in 1961 replacing Ike. I have now lived under fourteen Presidents. That statement makes me feel old but not too old to remember that special day in the fall when Dwight David Eisenhower came to Delaware, Ohio.

JOLE BLON

I first came to know about Jole Blon from the mystery novels of James Lee Burke. His writing domain is Southern Louisiana, New Orleans and Iberia. All mystery writers have a certain area of the country they write about.

Burke's description of the Bayou and area around it is unsurpassed. You can feel the evening breeze and the light rain in your face. The characters in his books are from the area and reflect the country and times they live in and were born in. Jole Blon is an old Cajun tune about the sweetheart that got away. Picture yourself in a concrete block, flat roofed crowded bar on a hot Saturday night somewhere along the Bayou. You came in to get drunk, have fun and listen to some music. You want to forget your life if only for a night. The fiddler is singing in French Creole and strumming the familiar tune, "Jole Blon"

Jole Blon   lovely blond

Jole Blon   lovely blond

You left me to go away with another

To get away lovely blond with another

I do you think I'm goin' to do know (direct French translation)

Lovely blond, lovely blond

I got drunk all night long

All night long lovely blond

As you know me, it's getting hard to think

Lovely blond, lovely blond

You left me to go away

Jole Blon, Jole Blon

If only, if only Jole Blon

You could have been mine

Life would have been different with you Jole Blon

Many musicians and singers were captivated by the music and words of Jole Blon. To get the real Cajun feel go to U tube and type in "Harry Choates/ Jole Blon." It was recorded in 1946.

To get Jole Blon in the original French Creole put "Waylan Jennings /Jole Blon" into U tube. Buddy Holly and Waylan recorded a version of Jole Blon in 1958 in a little recording studio in New Mexico. Even Bruce Springsteen recorded a version of the famous song. Each of the singers changed the words to better portray what they thought the song meant

If you're ever lucky enough to travel to New Orleans, stay at the Blake Hotel. It's on the corner of St. Charles Street. One of my special moments that make a life worthwhile was sitting in the lobby of the Blake Hotel one morning sipping a delicious cup of coffee while listening to the clang of the trolley rumbling up St. Charles Street toward the scenic Garden District.

Your first stop in the morning is Café Du Monde for coffee and Beignets. Nothing better, no refills on the coffee so slurp slowly. For lunch do the shrimp encrusted Poor Boy. For dinner try the New Orleans Gumbo. Any Gumbo made in New Orleans is worth the trip.

After all that and some tums, if you need them, look for the earthiest bar with the oldest musicians. After they finish their set, stand up with a twenty creased in your fingers and yell out, "Play Jole Blon." Then set back and listen to a true South Louisiana Cajun ballad. We have all had a Jole Blon at one time in our lives who got away. At the time we thought the experience was devastating but in hindsight it may have been a blessing.

KONNICHIWA

When my cousin heard we were going to Yellowstone for the summer, she mentioned that she had been there in the spring. She said there were many Japanese tourists there.

Since I was going to be a host in one of the dining rooms, I thought it would be friendly to learn a few Japanese words. I already knew "ohayou gozaimasu" which means good morning . Being from Ohio, ohayou was easy to remember because it was pronounced the same.

From reading James Michener's book, "Sayonara," I learned that sayonara means goodbye. I have a step-grandson in the Navy stationed in Japan. He has married a lovely Japanese girl and has two beautiful daughters. When he was home, I tried to impress him by letting him know I knew how to say hello and goodbye in Japanese. He gently informed me that sayonara is a personal goodbye like to a loved one.

A movie was made from the book "Sayonara," in 1957 starring Marlon Brando. There was a cute song that was created by Irving Berlin just for the movie. It went:

"Whisper Sayonara

But you needn't cry

Sayonara, if it must be so

Whisper Sayonara

Smiling as we go

No more we stop to see

Pretty cherry blossoms

No more we beneath the tree"

James Michener was a prolific writer. He had other books made into movies: "Hawaii," "Bridges of Toko-ri" and his most famous, "Tales of the South Pacific." Michener also wrote a book titled, "The Fires of Spring." It was autobiographical. The book was very interesting because it gave you a glimpse of the origin and persona of the man who wrote all those great novels.

In the late fifties, two other guys and I took a vacation to San Francisco. There was a beautiful Japanese girl from Hawaii who worked in the Japanese Tea Garden in Golden Gate Park. I struck up a friendship with her and visited her ever afternoon. I was too shy to ask her out. Now in my vintage years, I believe I missed the bus. The beautiful Japanese girl was my Jole Blon. I wonder what might have been, if only.

This old man has roamed way off the subject. Back to Konnichiwa. My wife found a book on Japanese sayings. We tried to learn some Japanese words on our long road trip to Yellowstone. Konnichiwa, which means hello, was the only greeting that survived.

While working in the Grant Village Dining Room many Asians frequented the restaurant. It was difficult for a novice like me to tell what country they were from. Finally, one evening a tall beautiful girl came into the dining room with flawless white skin. She looked just like the geisha girls I had seen in the movies. I said to myself, "this is the chance to use my Japanese." I boldly blurted out, "Konnichiwa." She quickly replied, "I'm Chinese."

That was my first and last foray into diplomacy using my foreign language skills.

JACK KEROUAC

On a cool March Saturday morning in the winter of 2013, the St. Petersburg Times in Florida printed a front-page story about the author, Jack Kerouac. The article had pictures and addresses of the house he lived in and the bar (The Flamingo) where he hung out. Kerouac died in St. Petersburg, Florida, in 1996 at the age of forty-six.

"On the Road" was the most famous book the author wrote. The book described his travels, by car, across this wide wonderful country of ours. His enthusiasm, joy and wonderment of the adventure of rolling across the country was captivating to the reader.

Kerouac's writings reflected his joy of living free to roam around this scenic country by car and not be anchored by a job or financial responsibility. He was what they called, "A Beatnik." A beatnik was a drop-out of society who scorned the values and status seeking lust of the 1940s and 1950s.

I was here back in those times and traveled around the country on a shoestring as he did. Since I enjoyed the adventure of my travels, I could identify with his philosophy. His books fueled my desire and enjoyment to my life. In fact, he gave a sort of validly to my existence.

We have wintered in St. Petersburg for the last twelve years. I have often wondered where the "Kerouac house" was but I never looked it up. On this special Saturday morning, I cut the article out of the paper and headed over to be reunited with my hero from the past. I visited the bar where he drank and bought a black tee shirt with a picture of him on the front and on the back of the tee shirt was the following:

"The only people for me are the mad ones, the ones who are mad to live, mad to talk, mad to be saved, desirous of everything at the same time, the ones who never yawn or say common place things, but burn, burn, burn like fabulous yellow roman candles exploding like spiders across the stars."

Jack Kerouac

WOW! I am really energized all over again. I have reconnected with a kindred spirit. I have got to share this experience with someone. It would be best if this someone was a Kerouac fan too. But who? Is there not someone left who could identify with my elation?

It is my opinion that those of us who have reached our senior years, have experienced that there is no one left to share our precious past recollections. Seniors should demand that our family and friends give us signed, notarized pledges on our birthdays and Christmases that the undersigned must listen to the recipient's opinions, stories and complaints without bitterness, condescendingness or falling asleep.

SUMMERTIME

When we were kids, summer was the best time of the year. School was out and we had the whole summer just to play. We could just drift from one joyous activity to another. Whatever the gang was up to.

Kids now-a-days have no time to drift. Everything is programmed: summer ball league, church camps, scout camps, swimming lessons, sleep overs, pizza parties and family vacations. School lets out one week into June and starts again the middle of August. What happened to summer?

In our day Porgy and Bess said it best:

"Summertime and the livin' is easy
The fish are jumpin' and the cotton is high
One of these mornings, you're going to rise up singing
You'll spread your wings and you'll take to the sky
But in that morning, ain't nothin' going to harm you
With Daddy and Mammy standin' by."

Our young lives were certainly secure as we headed for the swimming pool for another leisure day of fun. To be at the pool on a hot summer day. Nothing could top that.

The girls would be sitting on their towels tanning and talking girl talk which was a foreign language to us boys. The boys would be clowning around hoping to be noticed by the girls on the towels.

One sure way to get their attention was to do a cannonball close to them. For those ill-informed readers, a cannonball is when you jump off the side of the pool or diving board, pull your legs up and wrap your arms around your legs, forming a big ball. When you enter the water you hopefully make a big splash. It is especially pleasing if the blast of water sprays one of the girls. If the girl squeals and gives you a dirty look, then your mission is accomplished. The boys making the biggest splash were looked up to by the skinnier boys.

In thinking about this boyish ornery duty, I can't ever remember a girl doing a cannonball. There must be some profound epiphany to be learned here but it's beyond me. I wonder if now-a-days boys still cannonball and girls still squeal?

Before we leave the pools of yesteryear, we should give some thought to chlorine. When we were at the pool years ago, we were not supposed to open our eyes under water because the chlorine would make them hurt and sting. As irresponsible kids, the rule was not followed. My concern is that the chlorine of that era had unhealthy effect on our eyes that has ramifications to this day. Now here is the kicker, can we as poor unsuspecting seniors have a class action suit against the makers of this dastardly liquid? If any seniors out there want to spearhead this project, go for it. I only brought this subject up, so you know why you're tired all the time, your joints creak and your muscles ache. The doctors blame it all on arthritis, but we know it's because of chlorine.

In closing, can you remember how it felt to spend those calm, worry free days at the pool in the summer. Life was uncomplicated. We were free and life was good. The only thing that the girls had to worry about was a cannonball and the boys were not wired to worry. We never had it so good.

THE PREACHER WITH A GUN

On our western trip with the family in 2016, we were in Santa Fe on the Fourth of July at an Econo Lodge. I usually arise, early, so I stumbled down to the lobby for a cup of hot coffee.

There was a friendly group having a leisurely breakfast preparing for the Holiday in one of America's most beautiful historic cities.

I had toted a book with me to kill time until the rest of the tribe arose. I noticed that a gentleman was reading also. I asked him if what he was reading was good. He replied, "The best book ever." I then noticed that his book was the Bible. I said, "Good for you." That is what I always say when someone hits me with a reply that renders me speechless.

The Bible reader was dressed in jeans, a western shirt, a medium size turquoise belt buckle along with a nice pair of cowboy boots. As he got up to get a refill on his coffee, I noticed he was wearing a holster on his belt with a gun. The holster was located on the back of his hip where John Wayne used to wear his.

The Bible and the gun contradicted each other. In talking to him, he revealed that he was a preacher. He was from New Mexico and was holding a tent revival here in Sane Fe for a couple of days. He politely invited me and the rest of the family to join them that evening.

I find it hard to wrap my mind around the concept of a preacher with a gun. I know Clint Eastwood did it in "Pale Rider," but that was in the movies. I wonder if Clint wore a gun when he preached? That would deter worshipers from stealing from the collection plate.

We stayed at the Econo Lodge for a couple days enjoying the unique downtown area of Santa Fe with its splendid churches and adobe architecture. We had a chance to converse with the Preacher a few more times.

In my estimation when you carry a gun and meet up with someone else carrying a gun, your assumption is that the other person is going to use his gun. You must be prepared to use your gun. Therein lies your call to action.

The Preacher was a unique person who heard a different drummer. He belonged in the West where people are given more room to be different. The rewarding aspect about travel is that you meet all kinds of people in this great country of ours.

THE UNEXPLAINABLE

I am sitting in our livingroom in my big easy chair reading when I notice that the hall closet door is ajar. The door is usually closed. I make a special point of closing the closet door. Why is it ajar? Who would have opened the door?

Other quirky things have begun occurring around the house. When I am home alone in the evening unexplained creaking sounds emanate from the rooms, I am not in.

I have begun to wonder if our home is haunted. I don't believe in ghosts, but they seem to wait until I am alone before starting their antics. There could be one or more. They are not scary. They just like to play games.

One of the shenanigans they enjoy is to leave the garage door open at night. They know that the last thing I do before bed is to check to see if the garage door is closed. Are they teasing me?

They also delight in hiding things like the keys to my car, my cell phone or my billfold. They know those are the three items I need before leaving the house. When I frantically run around trying to find these incidentals, I can almost hear them giggling.

The sneaky buggers will go so far as to move my bath towel. When I get out of the shower wet. I must traipse across the bathroom to reclaim my towel.

I know it is a giant leap jumping from, "The unexplainable" to "Ghosts." I have no other explanations for these odd happenings. My wife does not seem to be bothered by these events. Maybe it's me.

LET UP AND LIGHT UP SMOKE-EM IF YOU GOT-EM

I have been thinking for years to create a story that would go with the above title. This saying dates back to (the big one,) "World War ll." Almost everyone smoked back then so when they took a break in the service they said, "Let up and light up. Smoke-um if you got-um."

During the War, I was young. My first smoke was corn cob silk rolled up in a piece of newspaper. I can't recommend it but you have to start somewhere. I was not into salvaging tobacco from Dad's old cigarette buts.

During the War cigarettes were scarce. The government sent all the cigarettes over to the troops. Dad had a cigarette rolling contraption. You started with the paper then poured tobacco in. The product came out pretty good. They were round, firm and fully packed. I wonder if they still make those cigarette rollers. With the popularity of smoking weed, those rollers would be in great demand.

Now-a-days in the modern services when they take a break from all their physical and mental duties, the drill instructor or officer in charge would yell out: "Let up, take a break, play with your cell phones. If you must smoke, get the hell away from here."

NOW THERES A HERO

We were moving from Delaware, Ohio, to South Carolina. The moving truck had moved all our possessions into the truck in one day. We stayed with our generous neighbor for the night. The following day, we cleaned the condo and took off in separate vehicles for South Carolina.

After staying the night with our neighbor, I decided to treat everyone to a McDonald's breakfast. I walked into McDonalds and got in line to order. In front of me was a short old man with gray hair. He wore a ball cap with a Navy ship insignia. I ask him what ship he served on. He said it was a landing craft or as they were called an LSTs. I asked him if he was in the European campaign? He replied, "Yes." My next question was, "Were you at Normandy?" My voice broke when I asked him this. He said he was. I could hardly believe that I was talking to a man that was there on D-Day. The date was late in October of 2013 and we were talking about D-Day, June 6, 1944. That was sixty-nine years earlier. Normandy is now a sacred, hallowed ground in honor of the greatest day in the history of warfare and the brave men who died there.

Andrew Higgins was the designer and builder of LSTs. This abbreviation stands for Landing Ship, Tank which were ships first developed during World War ll to support amphibious operations by carrying tanks, vehicles, cargo, and landing troops directly onto shores without using piers or docks. There were 23,358 of these landing crafts built. The ship held thirty-six soldiers. After the war Eisenhower said, "Higgins was the man who won the war for us." The ship was originally designed for oil companies to explore the Louisiana Bayou.

The friendly old man said that on that landing day his Captain told him to stand up and look around because he will never see another sight like this in his life. He said he stood up and looked at all the landing crafts headed towards the beach and all the monstrous ships in the background. He told me after Normandy he was assigned to the Pacific where he named four or five islands where he was involved in landing the troops.

There was a fortyish man standing behind me in a washed-out Marine tee shirt. He had been listening to our conversation. He looked at me and said, **"Now there's a hero."**

THE AUTHOR WISHES TO THANK

My incredible wife of fifty-six years, who followed me on this great adventure to Yellowstone National Park. Her experience there was much different than mine. She worked in a uniquely different department with an unexciting eight to five shifts. She never complained but was behind me in whatever I wanted to do or go.

It has taken me ten months to compose these stories and get them in shape for a book. A lot of that time I was sitting in a chair in front of the computer instead of working in the yard or helping with the household duties. She knew and accepted that "The Book" was my top priority and did not interfere.

I did not focus on my studies in school. My English grammar is abominable, and my spelling is worse than that. In my first book, I would yell out to my wife the word I had no idea how to spell and she would say the work then spell it out like someone in a spelling bee. With this creation, I used my cell phone and asked google. That worked out much better with less shouting taking place on the home front.

My wife spends her life bringing order to chaos. She certainly has chosen the right family. They say that behind every great man is a strong woman. I don't mean to infer that I am great, but this book would not have come into existence without my wife's understanding and help.

THE FOURTEENTH CHAPTER

I was going to stop writing after the Thirteenth Chapter, of the addendum, but my long departed sainted Mother would never have approved Thirteen Chapters. Mom was very superstitious. We, the family, thought it was cute but to our dismay some of that superstition has washed off on us.

Mother and her sisters when making house calls or visiting friends and family, would always make sure they left by the same door they entered. From my boyish translation of the deed, it meant that if you left by another door your spirit would remain in that dwelling. As a kid, I laughed at such a funny assumption. Now in my mature years, I find myself searching for the same door I entered when visiting people's homes.

When I was young, I would lay on the floor and watch television. Sometimes there was a rocking chair nearby. I would absentmindedly rock that empty rocker with my foot. This act would set my Mother off. An empty rocking chair rocking is a NO NO. Who knows what ghosts may be in that empty rocker? In our home now, we do not have a rocking chair, nor do I lay on the floor and watch television anymore. That problem has been solved.

When we were having family meals, If per chance I would drop a knife on the floor, Mom would immediately ask, which way the knife was pointing. It meant, she said, we were going to get company from that direction. Luckily the knife never landed so the blade was pointing straight up.

Mom was afraid of lightning, thunder and storms. She would set in the upstairs stairway with her eyes closed and her fingers crossed on both hands. The finger crossing thing was for luck to make it through this crisis. Later, she decided that just two fingers should be crossed because if one crossed four fingers that was a double cross. Logic and reason are a wonderful thing.

An open rain umbrella in the house was also a NO NO. I have never figured out why. Truthfully, I have never thought much about it, but I also never open an umbrella in a building. I do this just to be safe from all the demon's that may be out there looking for reasons to descend on my being.

Now I am sure all this superstition stuff sounds ridiculously funny to all you logical levelheaded people of the world. If you would have been raised in our family whose matriarch believed wholeheartedly all her life in the hereafter, the here before and the most of all the here now that we can't see but can feel. It is all a complicated process. You have to start by asking a ouija board questions about life and loved ones or you could ask to speak to someone that has passed on. Also, you could play "Rise Table Rise." That is where the participants sit around three sides of a table and chant, "rise table rise." If the group is serious about contacting an unearthly being, the empty side of the table mysteriously rises. I, myself, have never entered any of these Twilight Zone events but I do not necessarily dismiss them as hogwash.

I guess, after all, I do take after my superstitious mother in some ways. That is why there is a Fourteenth Chapter.